MARGRET & H. A. REY'S
Curious George
Visits the Library

Illustrated in the style of H. A. Rey by Martha Weston

HOUGHTON MIFFLIN HARCOURT
Boston New York

www.hmhco.com

The text of this book is set in Adobe Garamond.
The illustrations are watercolor and charcoal pencil, reproduced in full color.

Library of Congress Cataloging-in-Publication data is on file.

ISBN 978-0-544-11450-0

Manufactured in Mexico
RDT 10 9 8 7 6 5

4500605449

This is George.

He was a good little monkey and always very curious.

Today George and his friend the man with the yellow hat were at the library.

George had never been to the library before. He had never seen so many books before, either. Everywhere he looked, people were reading.

Some people read quietly to themselves.

But in the children's room the librarian was reading out loud.

It was story hour!
George loved stories. He sat down with a group of children to listen.
The librarian was reading a book about a bunny.
George liked bunnies.

Behind the librarian was a book about a dinosaur. George liked dinosaurs even more. He hoped she would read it next.

George tried to sit quietly and wait for the dinosaur book to be read.

But next the librarian read a book about a train.

But sometimes it is hard for a little monkey to be patient.

When the librarian started a story about jungle animals, George could not wait any longer. He had to see the dinosaur book.

He tiptoed closer.

"Look, a monkey!" shouted a girl.

The librarian put her finger to her lips. "We must be quiet so everyone can hear," she said nicely.

"But there's a monkey!" said a boy.

The librarian nodded and smiled. "Mmm-hmm," she agreed.

When she finished reading the jungle story,
the librarian reached for the dinosaur book.
Where did it go?
And where was George?

George was all ready to take the dinosaur book home and read it with his friend when another book caught his eye . . .

This book was about trucks.
George wanted to take it home, too!
And here was a book about elephants.
George loved elephants. He added it to his pile.

11

George found so many good books, he soon had more than he could carry. He leaned against a shelf to rest.

Squeak, went the shelf.

"Shhh!" said a man.

Squeak, went the shelf again – and it moved! Why, it wasn't really a shelf after all. George had found a special cart for carrying books.

What luck! Now George could carry all the books he wanted.
He rolled the cart between the shelves and stacked up books
about boats and kites and baking cakes. He climbed higher to reach
books about cranes and planes.

At last George had all the books he could handle. He couldn't wait to head home and start reading. And right in front of him was a ramp leading to the door. George was curious. Could he roll the cart all the way home?

Down the ramp George went. The cart rolled faster and faster.

"Stop!" a library volunteer shouted. "Come back here with my cart!"

But George was too excited to listen. The cart was picking up speed, and George was having fun!

Until – CRASH! – George and the cart ran
smack into a shelf of encyclopedias.
Books flew up in the air.
And so did George! He landed in a big pile
right between O and P.

"Oh no!" moaned the volunteer when he saw the mess George had made. "How am I going to put away all of these books?"

"I'd like to borrow this one," said a boy from story hour. "And I'll take this one," said a girl.

With help from George and the children,
the books were sorted in no time. Soon there
was just a small pile of George's favorites left.

"Would you like to take those books home with you?" the volunteer asked George. Then he took George to a special desk and helped him get his very own library card.

George was holding his brand-new card when his friend arrived with
a stack of books of his own. "There you are, George!" he said.
"I see you are all ready to check out."

George and his friend gave their books to the librarian.

She smiled when she saw George's pile. "I was wondering where this
dinosaur book went," she said. "It's one of my favorites, too."

The librarian stamped the books and handed them back to George.

With his books under one arm,
George waved goodbye to the
volunteer, the librarian, and
the children from story hour.

"Come see us again, George,"
the librarian said, waving back.
"Enjoy your books!"

And he did.

The end.